For Sha *with loads of love*

A story to introduce 'The Moldau' by Smetana

Editor: Robin Norman
Illustrations: Gilly Marklew
Design and Layout: Glide Design
Cd recording issued under license from Sanctuary Records Group Ltd.

Published 2005

BRING CLASSICAL MUSIC TO LIFE! FOR HOME OR SCHOOL

"As the I.T. teacher in a primary school in New Zealand, I am constantly looking for material that will stimulate, interest and if I'm lucky, excite and inspire my students. I can honestly say that the six stories in this series have exceeded my expectations and I have found them to be one of the most valuable resources I have used to date.

The books have something to offer to children from years 1 to 8 (the full primary school age range here in New Zealand) and it never ceases to amaze me how much they inspire the children. The combination of story with illustration and music is a great I.T. resource and the children create descriptive text, as well as art work, within the computer art programs available, and slide shows ranging from simple to complex.

The wonderfully inventive language they use to describe their work is reflective of what they are seeing and hearing within the stories and now the children are requesting other classical music pieces for their own original creations. Fantastic!"

Sharon Gardner, I.T. Teacher
Koputaroa School, Levin, New Zealand

"Story time is always special, but what a wonderful experience this was! Our two young sons, aged 5 and 3, were completely captivated by this series. They were wide-eyed with delight as they were able to hear in the music what was happening in the stories.

After a number of listenings, they were able to hear the music telling the story and painting pictures in their heads. Afterwards, I was plagued with requests for more!

I hope that the series continues to expand as this is something I'm sure we can use again and again to build on the children's understanding and love of music."

Penny Hill, Parent
Bury St. Edmunds, Suffolk

ABOUT THE BOOK

These books are designed to be used as part of your scheme of work for music, literacy and art and will particularly help generalists, as they are straight forward, interesting and fun to use. At home they become a fantastic alternative to traditional storytime.

If you ask children what they think of classical music they often say "It's boring." That's an understandable reaction. Classical music doesn't have the 'immediacy' of pop, rock, rap etc. It lacks a constant, even beat, often lacks lyrics and is usually longer than the average pop song.

However pieces such as The Sorcerer's Apprentice usually prove very popular with young children. Why? Because they have strong contrasting dynamics, are very descriptive, and best of all, they have a story. It is the story, particularly when combined with illustrations, that is the instant attraction.

Many pieces of classical music either do not have a story at all, or have an inappropriate one – too old, too complicated, too scary or simply too uninteresting. This series uses original stories written specifically for young children and inspired by short interesting pieces of music from a variety of different cultures. Although the stories are original, they bear some association with the title and flavour of the music.

HOW TO USE THIS BOOK AND CD

- Play the CD straight through and read the story at the same time
- In the book you will see a number of CD counter indications. This tells you when to proceed to the next part of the story
- Alternatively read the story through first then play the CD and this time just look at the pictures so you feel suspended by the music in the story
- Enjoy!

About 'The Moldau' or 'Vltava' from 'Ma Vlast'

Smetana was a Czech composer. He lived from 1824 – 1884 and is strongly romantic and nationalist in feeling, sometimes referred to as The Father of Bohemian Music. Ma Vlast (My Fatherland) is a cycle of six symphonic poems that depict the landscape and the spirit of Bohemia – a symphonic poem being an orchestral piece in one movement with a literary emphasis. 'Vltava' is the second of the six.

The music follows the course of the river as it flows through the woods with their hunters, then past a wedding. At dusk the sylphs and nymphs dance, then we hear the sound of the rapids of St. John and finally the river flows into the Elbe. The beautiful, well-known main theme is said to be derived from a Swedish folk-song.

Now enjoy the story!

CD ON

00.25

A heavy whiteness coats the land.
Layer on layer on layer of snow.
The river gleams – a ribbon of ice
Blocking the sounds from far below.
"Can't see the way!" cries a watery voice.
"Can't see the way to flow."

01.01

Billy listens, frowning, thinking,
"I will guide the way," he calls.
So on the surface Billy skates
While deeper down the water crawls,
And trees with bony branches point
From underneath their winter shawls.

01.39

Surging, sliding, pushing, gliding
Along the river towards the sea,
There's just the scrape of skates on ice
And watery whispers, "Set me free."
Then even when the darkness gathers
Billy sings out, "Follow me!"
But deep inside his heart is sinking.
What if the water can never run free?

02.11

Surging, sliding, pushing, gliding
Along the river towards the sea
Glinting skates and scratching ice
And Billy...lonely as can be.

The night time air is shuddering, shaking,
Cracking, thudding, sharp and strong.
But no, it's celebration noise,
A ploo-pop, pounding sing-a-long.

03.27

Trees are swaying, music playing,
Night time creatures dance around.
"Take heart!" they call to Billy.
"Then you'll find what we have found."

They line the river, poised and straight,
Saluting trees in marching drill.
And Billy feels quite sad to leave
And skate in air that hangs so still.

The echo of the party races,
Chasing Billy with its beat.
A gentle pulse, the sweetest sound
That keeps the dance in Billy's feet.

It's more than just an echo though.
A face! Yes, that's what Billy sees.
Then more and more, with smiles, they step out
From the cover of the trees.

05.18

Now the music is dissolving
Folding into dusky grey
And Billy wonders how much longer
Till the night turns back to day.
But then he hears the water's anxious murmur,
"Are you going to stay?"
"Yes," he answers, skating harder.
"Yes, I'm with you all the way."

06.08

Those words of Billy's shiver
In an arc across the granite sky,
And Billy sees a flicker
Like a starry nightlight, way up high.
Then sprigs and sprays and showers
Of sparkling stars come floating by.

07.09

"I never knew," says Billy,
As the stardrops fall in beads of hail,
"That you could light the way along a river
With a glitter trail."

08.00

There's *something* in the air!

There's *something* in the air.
There's *something* out there.
There's *something* out there!
What is it? Whatever can it be?
Something coming nearer?
Is it the sea?
Is it the sea?

The *something* has gone
In a brushing, rushing sweep.
The air is quite still now.
The ice has grown deep.
But where is the water?
Has the river gone to sleep?

09.06

Surging, sliding, pushing, gliding
Along the river towards the sea,
And Billy's sinking heart still singing
"Follow me! Yes follow me!"

09.51

What is wrong?
The surface rocks.
Danger blocks
The way ahead.

A beaver dam.
It goes so deep.
It reaches high, it stretches wide.
It leaves nowhere to tread.

So Billy stops and stares and thinks
And feels his heart fill up with dread.
The water cannot move at all.
It's sunk into the riverbed.
And still it rocks,
And still it rocks,
And still it blocks the way ahead.

10.30

And now the trees have made an arch
Entwined their branches with the dam,
And Billy somehow finds his voice
And shouts out loud, "I'm strong, I AM!
And I can fight, and I have friends,
And they will help unblock the dam!"

11.05

Then there's a rumbling and a crumbling.
And the beavers out in grand parade.
They scratch and chip and slowly unpick,
And unpack and unblock the dam that they made.

The water will flow now,
The fear will all go now,
The daylight will grow now
And night time will fade.

And in the distance Billy sees
The sight he thought he'd never see.
The vicious, vice-like grip of ice
Has set the water free.
And on it flows, and on and on
And out into the sea.

12.02

"I've done it!" Billy calls with pride.
"Is that because I tried and tried?"

A heavy whiteness coats the land
Layer on layer on layer of snow.
The silken river swirls and swishes,
Full of rhythm, full of flow.

"I've found the way," said a watery voice.
"And I have too!" a voice replied.
But did it come from far below?
Or did it come from deep inside?
That's what Billy wants to know.
That's what Billy wants to know.

END